Annual 2018

This book is about

_____ and Bing!

(you!)

(you!)

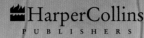

HarperCollins
PUBLISHERS

ACAMARFILMS

Copyright © 2017 Acamar Films Ltd
First published in the UK in 2017 by HarperCollins Children's Books, a division of
HarperCollins Publishers Ltd, 1 London Bridge Street, London SE1 9GF
10 9 8 7 6 5 4 3 2 1
ISBN: 978-0-00-823604-5
The Bing television series is an Acamar Films production, co-produced in association
with Brown Bag Films and adapted from the original books by Ted Dewan.
Written by Lydia Barram, Nicola Carthy, and Emma Drage
Edited by Lydia Barram, Amelia Hepworth, Freddie Hutchins and An Vrombaut
Designed by Claire Yeo
A CIP catalogue record for this title is available from the British Library.

MIX
Paper from
responsible sources
FSC
www.fsc.org
FSC® C007454

FSC™ is a non-profit international organisation established to promote
the responsible management of the world's forests. Products carrying the
FSC label are independently certified to assure consumers that they come
from forests that are managed to meet the social, economic and
ecological needs of present and future generations,
and other controlled sources.

Find out more about HarperCollins and the environment at
www.harpercollins.co.uk/green

Contents

All about Bing – and me!

Hello!

This is **Bing**, and this is **Flop**, who looks after him.

And this is where they live!

This is **me**, and this is **my house!**

I live with

....

Here they are!

6

Bing likes **lots** of things.

He likes his **yellow wellies.**

He likes his **penguin cup.**

He likes his **toy cars.**

But he **loves** Hoppity Voosh!

I like lots of things too!

I like

....
I also like

....

I like ....

And
I love

....

7

Bing has lots of **friends**.

This is Sula. Sula is Bing's **best friend!** She lives with Amma, and her favourite colour is **pink**.

Woo-hoo!

This is Pando. He likes to run around in his **pants!**

And here are Bing's **cousins**, Coco and Charlie!

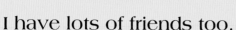

I have lots of friends too.

My **very** best friend is ...., who looks like this.

My other friends are

Bing and his friends all like to play **together**.

They play with their **favourite** toys. →

 Hoppity Voosh

 **Fairy Hippo**

Rainbow Fairy Mouse

 Bulabaloo

They play **Big Bad Wolf**

and **musical statues.**

Sometimes they go to the **park** to feed the **ducks.**

Charlie is only a baby so they play **special** Charlie games with him.

My favourite toy is

....

My friend's favourite toy is

....

And our **favourite** thing to do together is

....

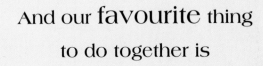

9

Something for Sula

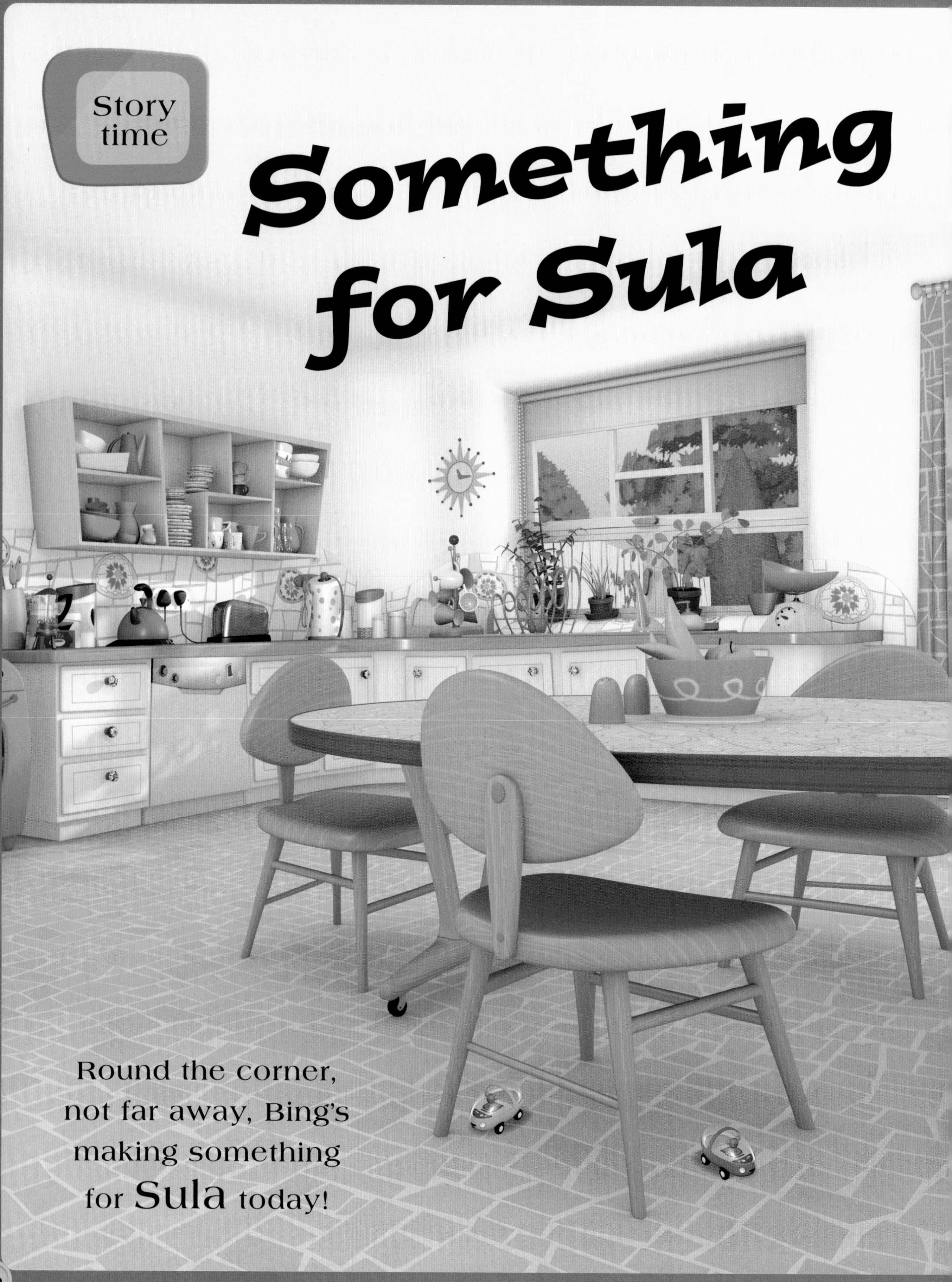

Round the corner,
not far away, Bing's
making something
for **Sula** today!

A card has just arrived through the letterbox. It's for Bing – from Sula!

"Ohhhh," says Bing. "I love it! Can I make one for Sula, Flop?"

"Good idea," agrees Flop. "What will you need to make it?"

"Erm... some pink card. Sula likes pink!"

Bing gets his crayons and begins drawing a picture on the card.

"What is it, Bing?" asks Flop.

"Me!" says Bing.
"And Sula, with
her **magic
fairy wand**."

"Lovely.
What's next?"

"**Some
shinies!**" cries Bing.
"Sula loves shinies!"

Bing fetches the shiny decorations from
the drawer and Flop hands him the glue.

*Splotch!
Splotch!
Splotch!*

"There!" says Bing, when
he's stuck on his shinies.
"Sula will like that!"

"Indeed!" laughs Flop.
"What's next?"

"Erm... I know - pasta!"

"OK! Would Sula like butterfly pasta, or twirly pasta?"

"Oh, butterflies! Sula LOVES butterflies!" Bing adds some more glue to his picture.

Splat!
Splot!
Splotch!

He sticks the butterfly pasta onto the glue, and sits back to see what it looks like.

"More glue!" cries Bing.

Splotch!
Splish!
Splotch!

"Steady, Bing. You only need a little bit of glue for it to work," says Flop. "Now – what's next?"

"Hmm. Feathers!"

Flop finds the feathers, and Bing adds **more** glue to his picture to stick the feathers on.

Splosh!
Splosh!
Splash!

THERE.

The picture is finished. It looks beautiful!

But something is missing.

"Oh - Sula's magic wand needs a **jewel** on the top!"

Bing squeezes the glue bottle ready for the jewel – but this time, nothing comes out!

"The glue's stuck!"

Bing keeps squeezing and squeezing, but then –

SPLOOSH!

– the glue comes out in one big rush all over Bing's picture!

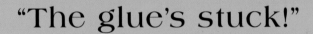

"Oh no!" cries Bing. "The glue's gone everywhere, Flop! It's all **yucky now!**"

"Oh dear. Yes, sometimes it does that, Bing, but don't worry – it's no big thing."

"Oh, but Flop! Sula won't love her picture now."

"Well – are you sure, Bing? Maybe it's just not finished yet? Is there something else you could add that Sula likes?"

Bing thinks for a moment.

"Oh yes! Sula likes sparkles!"

He rushes to get some glitter. Silver will look great on Sula's picture! Bing tips the glitter over the great big glue splodge. It sticks! And it looks wonderful.

"Look, Flop! It's beautiful!" smiles Bing. "Sula's going to love it. Can we give it to her now?"

"Indeed!"

If you think your picture's all yucky, maybe it's just not finished yet!

Let's make a pasta picture frame!

You will need:

- an apron
- old newspapers
- a sheet of paper
- a sheet of card the same size, with a rectangle cut out of the middle – a grown-up can help you do this!
- a pencil
- crayons
- pasta shapes – butterflies, shells, or twirly swirls – choose your favourite!
- glue
- poster paint
- shinies, glitter, or anything else you'd like to decorate your frame with

Bing made a super-special picture for his friend, Sula. Now let's make something nice that you can send to *your* best friend!

What to do:

1. Cover your table with newspapers and put on an apron so you don't get all sticky!

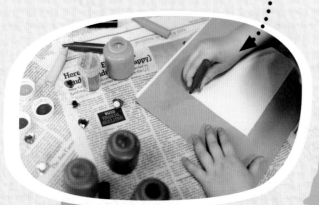

2. Place the card over your sheet of paper, lining up the edges, and draw a pencil line around the inside.

3. Take the card away and draw a picture inside the pencil line. Now colour it in! You can write your name on it too, if you like.

4. Now splodge some glue onto the card frame and stick on lots of pasta shapes. You can make a nice pattern with them or stick them on higgledy-piggledy.

5. Choose your favourite colour and paint over the pasta shapes and the frame. You can add some glitter or stick on some shinies too!

6. When you're finished and it's all dry, splodge some more glue around the edges of your picture and stick the frame down on top.

Wow!

Now you have a beautiful picture you can give to your friend. Maybe they can hang it on their wall, like in a gallery!

Friends... they're a Bing thing!

Bing has lots of friends – Sula, Pando, Coco and Charlie! Here are some of the things Bing loves about his friends.

Playing together

Bing and Coco love to play dressing up together. Bing is Super Magic Lion King Bing and Coco is Princess Coco-ca-pono! What do you like dressing up as?

Being brave

If you're scared of doing something, you can watch your friend do it first. If they like it, then you might like it, too!

Sharing secrets

Your best friend is the friend you can tell all your secrets to. Shhhhhh! Who do you share your secrets with?

Cheery-up hugs

Sometimes you might feel a bit sad, but that's okay – your friends can **cheer you up** with a **big hug**!

Charlie games

Bing's cousin Charlie is only little, so Bing has to think of special games to play with him. Charlie games are **noisy** – and **fun**, even if you're **big** like Bing! **Do you have a friend who is littler than you?**

Putting on a show

Bing and his friends **love** **singing** and **dancing** – and doing acrobatics! If you get a little bit shy when it's your turn, don't worry - **your friends can help you!**

Being a good friend

Having friends is lots of fun!

But sometimes, Bing and his friends don't have fun when they play together. Sometimes they can get angry or jealous – or even under-the-blankety...

Sharing

It's nice to share with your friends. You can even share your favourite things... but it's okay to keep your favouritest favourite to yourself.

Asking

If your friend feels a bit under-the-blankety, you can ask them what's wrong. Showing you care can help make them feel a lot better.

Listening

When your friend is talking, it's good to listen. Shhhhh – can you hear what they are saying?

Taking turns

Sometimes you **both** want to do the **same** thing at the **same** time! Waiting is hard, but it's no big thing – if you take turns, **you'll both have a go!**

Angry clouds

If you and your friends are feeling **angry**, try blowing all your angry up at the clouds. Go outside, find a cloud – and **blow!** Bye bye, angry!

Best friends

Bing and his friends **love** each other very much. Make sure you tell your friends how much you love them – **and see them smile!**

A - Z with Bing

A is for Amma

Amma **looks after** Sula. When Bing and his friends are at the crèche, Amma looks after them too! Amma is very good at growing things in her garden, like beautiful flowers and nobbly potatoes.

B is for Bubble Duck

Bubble Duck **makes bubbles** for Bing's bath. Bubbles burst when you touch them, but **popping** bubbles is all part of the fun!

C is for Carroty bagels

Bagels are bread rolls with holes in their middles. Bing's favourite bagels have crunchy carrots inside. They're **yummy-delicious**!

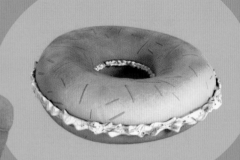

D is for Digger

Diggers are BIG machines that can make holes in the ground for planting trees – or even building a house! Bing's favourite digger is an excavator.

E is for Eggy

Bing loves his Eggy! You can make your own Eggy Head with egg shells and cress seeds. They need **light** and **water** to grow – but not too much!

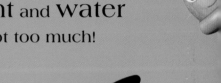

F is for Flop

Flop takes care of Bing. If Bing is feeling under-the-blankety, Flop always knows what to do. Flop loves Bing very much – and Bing loves Flop too.

G is for Goggles

Goggles stop you getting water in your eyes when you go swimming. Bing wears his special blue goggles when he goes splashing in the padding pool.

H is for Hoppity Voosh

Hoppity Voosh is Bing's favourite superhero. Bing and Hoppity go vooshing together. The garden is the best place to voosh because there is lots of space to fly really high!

Knack

Round the corner, not far away, Bing and his friends are making noises today...

Slurp slurp

Peeeep peeep

"Ah! Finished my juice!" says Pando.

"Finished!" says Sula.

"All gone!" says Bing.

"You three make some interesting whistly noises with your juice boxes," laughs Flop.

"Padget can whistle **without** a juice box," says Sula.

♪ **Fweeet**  "How do you do that, Padget?" asks Bing.

"Well, first you put your lips together, then you take a **big breath**... and then you **blow** very gently."

pbbbbbsssss

Pfffffft

"Ooh," says Bing. "It's hard!"

Flop has a go, too.

♪ **Peeeeep**

"**You** can do it, Flop!" says Bing.

"I can, Bing. But not as well as Padget. She's got quite the **knack** for it."

"What's a knack?"

"A knack is a special thing you can do," says Flop.

"Have **I** got a knack, Flop?"

"Sure! Everybody's got a knack, Bing. You've just got to find it."

"I've got one!" says Sula. "I've got a **knack** for **trumpet-blowing**! Watch..."

BRRRRRRRPPPPPP!!!

Bing and Pando have a go, but trumpet-blowing is **hard**! They don't have a knack for it like Sula.

Oooooooooo

Pfffffffffff

ffffffffffffffff

"I've got a knack too," says Pando. "I can do this...watch!"

Pando lies down on the grass and starts twirling round and round.

"Very good!" laughs Flop.

"I'm going to try it," shouts Bing.

"Me too!" giggles Sula.

Bing and Sula lie down on the grass.

They try really hard... but they just can't spin like Pando.

"Ohhhh. I want my own special knack." says Bing.

"You do have one, Bing," says Flop.

"Where? How do I know what my knack is?"

"Well, you just keep trying new things and you'll find it."

"Hmmm," says Bing. "I know! How about this..."

Bing grabs one foot and balances on his other leg.

"Ah! You've got the knack for one-foot-standing!" says Flop.

I've got that knack, too!

And me!

"It looks like everybody has the knack for one-foot-standing," smiles Flop. "But don't worry Bing. You'll find your knack – have another go."

"Hmmmm," Bing thinks really hard about what his knack might be.

"Oh! I can do this!"

Bing does a roly-poly on the grass.

"I can do that too!" says Sula.

"**And me!**" says Pando.

Pando and Sula start roly-polying with Bing, all around the garden!

But then...

Owwwwwwwww!

Oh dear! Pando roly-polies right onto Bing's ear.

"Are you ok, Bing?" asks Flop.

"Ohh... **Sorry, Bing,**" says Pando. "I didn't know your ears were there!"

"Oh, poor Bing," says Sula.

Everyone gives Bing a big hug.

"Feel any better, Bing?" asks Padget.

Yup...

POP

"What was that noise?" asks Sula.

"What noise?" says Bing.

"That popping noise!"

"What, this?" Bing lifts his ears up one by one...

POP

POP

"My ears went pop!" laughs Bing.

"I'm going to try it!" giggles Sula.

Oh! My ears won't do it!

Neither will mine!

"Oh! Is that my knack, Flop?"

"Yes! Looks like you've found your knack. Good for you, Bing Bunny!"

Everybody's got their own special knack – what's yours?

More about Bing – and me!

Bing is a **boy** bunny, and he has **black** hair and **green** eyes.

Bing likes wearing his **RED** dungarees best, and his **favourite** toy is Hoppity Voosh.

Vooooooshhh!

This is a picture Bing drew of himself – a **self-portrait**.

My hair colour is

....

And I have ....
coloured eyes.

My **favourite** thing to wear is

....

and my **favourite** toy is

....

Draw your **self-portrait** here!

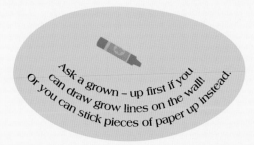

Ask a grown – up first if you can draw grow lines on the wall! Or you can stick pieces of paper up instead.

Flop measures how **tall** Bing is by drawing a **grow line** on the wall. You have to do it properly – like this...

Feet flat? **Head up?** **Ears down?**

Yup! **Yup!** **Yup!**

How tall are YOU getting? Can someone measure for you?

On...................., I was...............high – but on...................., I was ....high!
(date) (date)

On...................., I was...............high – but on...................., I was ....high!
(date) (date)

On...................., I was...............high – but on...................., I was ....high!
(date) (date)

Is Bing taller than his friends?

This is how **big** Bing's hand is:

This is how **big** my hand is: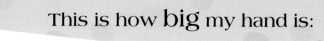

And this is how **big** his foot is!

And this is my foot!

Flop helped me draw around them!

It can be tricky to draw around your own hands and feet, so ask for help if you need it!

Bing can do something **special** with his ears – he can make them go...

POP!

POP!

When you can do something special, it's called a **knack**.

Pando's knack is spinning around on the ground really **fast**.

Don't get too dizzy, Pando!

My **knack** is

....

....

and this is a picture of me doing it!

Does your friend have a knack too?

Put a picture of them here.

Let's get dressed!

What are Bing and his friends going to wear today? Let's help them get dressed!

Bing is going outside in the rain! He'll need to wear something to help him stay dry.

Sula is going to play in the paddling pool. She needs to wear something she can get splish-splashy in!

Coco likes to play dressing-up.
Who will she be today?
Princess Coco-ca-pono!

Can you choose one thing from each list for Bing, Sula and Coco to wear?

1.

Yellow wellies

Twirly tutu

Swimsuit

2.

Winter coat

Princess jewels

Armbands

3.

Tiara

Beach ball

Umbrella

While you were choosing, Pando got dressed all by himself!

Do you like his outfit?

What about you? What would **you** like to wear today?

Choose your **favourite** outfit and get a grown-up to take a **picture** of you in it so you can stick it here!

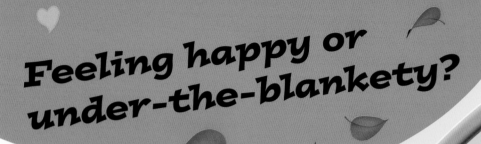

Feeling happy or under-the-blankety?

Proud

Bing has learned how to skateboard. **Wheeee!** Learning something new can make you feel proud!

How are you

Proud

Happy

Scared

Happy

Playing a favourite game with a friend can make you happy. Bing loves to go **vooshing** with Hoppity and Sula!

Scared

Bing doesn't like it when it's **all dark,** but using a torch to see makes the night-time much less scary. Exploring in the dark can even be **fun**!

Sorry

When Bing breaks Flop's phone he hides it so Flop won't see it. Bing knows it was the **wrong** thing to do, and feels sorry. Telling Flop makes him feel better.

feeling today?

Sorry

Angry

Excited

Angry

Coco's knocked over Bing's tower! So Bing messes up her rainbow. Now they **both** feel angry! Flop helps them find a way to play together – by building a special **rainbow tower!** Then they don't feel angry anymore.

Excited

Bing and Sula can't wait to watch the **fireworks**. Seeing something new can be very exciting! What makes you feel excited?

A - Z with Bing

I is for Icicles

When it is really, **really** cold outside, you might find an icicle. Icicles are made when drippy water gets **so cold** that it freezes. If you touch an icicle your hand will feel icy-cold. **Brrr!**

J is for Juice

Bing's **favourite** kind of juice is made from carrots. Yum! He likes to take **carrot juice** to Amma's crèche in his Hoppity Voosh lunchbox.

K is for Kite

It is hard to fly a kite on your own. You have to do it **together!** Bing does the running and Pando does the vooshing, and then – **whoosh!** – Bing's kite flies up, up, up in the sky.

Whoosh!

L is for Leaves

In the autumn, the leaves change colour and **fall down** from the trees. Flops says it's because the trees are **getting ready** for winter. Bing likes to catch the falling leaves!

Prrrr!

Prrrr!

M is for Mitten and her kittens

When cats have babies they are called kittens. They are so tiny! When Mitten the cat and her baby kittens are happy they make a purring sound. Prrrr! Prrrr!

N is for Noisy fireworks

Fireworks make beautiful patterns in the night sky. Ooh! Ahh! But bangy rockets can be very noisy. Flop makes Bing some special earmuffs so he can enjoy the fireworks without the super-loud bangs!

O is for Owly Nightlight

Owly is Bing's special nightlight. Bing doesn't like it when it is all dark so he needs his Owly Nightlight to feel cosy at bedtime.

P is for Penguin Cup

Penguin Cup is Bing's very own drinking cup. When Flop is poorly, Bing lends him his Penguin Cup and makes him a special drink with squeezy lemon and honey.

Let's make some party food!

Bing's friends are all coming over for a **party!** Let's help Bing and Flop make some **yummy-delicious** party food.

Pando's Squirmy Caterpillars

✴ What to do: ✴

- Wash the celery and cut the sticks in half, lengthways. A grown-up can help you with this. Fill the hollow part up with cream cheese.

- Place the grapes in a line on top of the cream cheese until it's nearly full up. When you get to the end, stick on one last grape to make a head!

- Now we need to give the caterpillar a face! Put two dots of cream cheese on the head, then stick a mini choc chip or a raisin on each dot. Oh – he's looking at you!

You will need:

- green and red grapes
- celery
- cream cheese
- mini choc chips or raisins

Hello caterpillar!

Charlie's Icy Rainybow Blocks

You will need:

- some colourful fruit
  – try strawberries, orange, mango, kiwi, blueberries
- a fork or blender
- a spoon
- an ice-cube tray

What to do:

- Wash and peel your fruit and cut it into small pieces, then use a fork to smash it so it's all squidgy. Or you could ask Brenda the Blender to help!

- Spoon the fruit into the ice-cube tray and press it down into all the corners.

- Put the tray in the freezer and leave it until tomorrow. When you're ready to eat them, pop your Rainybow Blocks out onto a plate.

Sula's Sparkly Star Sandwiches

You will need:

- sliced bread
- jam
- butter or spread
- a star-shaped cookie cutter
- hundreds and thousands
- a plate

What to do:

- Take two slices of bread. Spread some jam on one and then stick them together. Now spread some butter on top.

- Use your cookie cutter to cut star shapes out of your sandwich. The leftover bits around the edges are yummy-delicious too!

- Pour out some hundreds and thousands onto a plate, then dip the buttery side of your stars into them, one by one. Wow – they're sparkly!

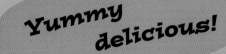

Yummy delicious!

45

Party time!

Hooray! It's time for the party. Bing, Sula, Coco and Pando have all brought their toys to the party too – but where have they gone?

Can you help find them?

See if you can find:

Hoppity Voosh

Fairy Hippo

Talkie Taxi

Rainbow Fairy Mouse

Oh – and Bing wants Eggy to come to the party too! Can you see him anywhere?

Found everything?

Good for you!

Bulabaloo

Pink Duckie

Sleepover

Round the corner, not
far away, Bing and Coco
share bedtimes today...

"OK," says Flop. "Teeth brushed?"

"Yup!"

"Jamas on?"

"Yup!"

"Now it's time to vooooosh!" says Bing.

"No - now it's time to play the **Goodnight Game**," says Coco.

"Well," says Flop. "Everybody's bedtimes are different. But you're supposed to get bedtimes all **mixed up** on a sleepover. So why don't we voosh AND play the Goodnight Game?"

"For the Goodnight Game, we need the **Rainbow Fairy Mice**," says Coco. "I can't sleep without them."

Bing nods. "I can't sleep without Hoppity."

Coco shows all her Rainbow Mice to Bing.

Sky

Scarlet

Brooke

Fern

Amber

Honey

Violet

"There's something special about Amber," says Coco. "But you'll find out later."

"Now let's do vooshing!" calls Bing.

"Hold on!" says Coco. "We haven't played the Goodnight Game yet. Now the Rainbow Fairy Mice have to say goodnight to everything in the room!"

"But...why?" asks Bing.

"Cause it's the Goodnight Game!" says Coco.

She gathers up her Fairy Mice
and turns to the chest of drawers.

"Goodnight Chest of Drawers,"
she says in her Rainbow Fairy
Mice voice. "Goodnight
Wardrobe... Goodnight Toys,
g'night Rug, g'night Light,
g'night Books..."

"And goodnight all the
other stuff. Now it's
vooshing time!"

Bing and Coco run about vooshing and laughing. When they've finished, Flop asks, "So we've done the Goodnight Game and we've done vooshing... What's next?"

"Bedtime story!" yells Bing.

"Bedtime kisses!" shouts Coco.

"Let's mix them up!" says Flop.

Bedtime kisses means Coco needs to kiss each of her Rainbow Fairy Mice in turn and wish them goodnight. She starts with Violet.

"Goodnight Violet... mwah! Now you do it, Bing."

Bing kisses Violet. "Goodnight Violet".

"Goodnight Scarlet... mwah."

"Goodnight Scarlet."

"Goodnight Honey... mwah!"

"Goodnight Fairy Mouses!"

Can we have the bedtime story now, Flop?"

"Oh – can I get a drink of water first please, Flop?"

"Ok!" says Flop. "You two get comfy in bed and I'll get the water."

Coco and Bing jump into bed.

"Move over, Bing!"

"Ooh Coco – your feet are cold!"

"I'm going to turn on my Owly Nightlight now," says Bing.

"No! Wait – I need to show you Amber's **special power!**" says Coco. "Here – you take Amber, and I'll turn off the light."

"Um…OK…" says Bing.

"Ready?" asks Coco.

She turns off the light.

"Oh! Oh no! I don't like it!" says Bing. "It's all dark!"

"Oh!" says Flop, coming back in with the water. "Why's it so dark?"

"It **needs** to be dark so you can see Amber's special power more properly!" says Coco.

"Look!"...and she presses a button on the Rainbow Fairy Mouse.

"Ohhhhh!" whispers Bing. "She's all **orangey!**"

"See? I told you you'd love it, Bing! Amber's **my** nightlight!"

"Owly's **my** nightlight! Flop – can we have **both** our nightlights on?"

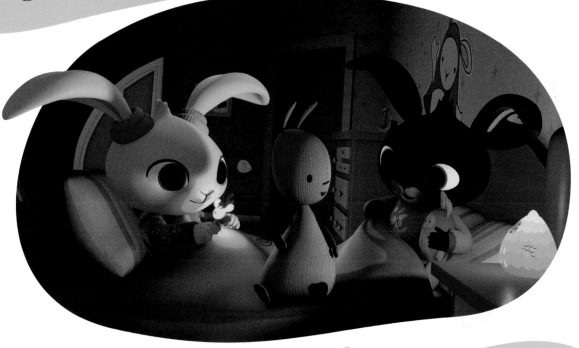

"Sure!" says Flop. "Now – who's ready for a bedtime story?"

Sleepovers... they're a **Bing** thing.

A - Z with Bing

Q is for Quacky ducks

Bing and Sula go to the **park** to feed the quacky ducks in the pond. **Wak-wak!** You need to stand **statue-still** to feed the ducks so you don't scare them away.

R is for Rainybow

You **might** see a rainbow in the sky when it is sunny and rainy at the same time. Bing calls them rainybows. Bing and Sula paint a **big**, beautiful rainybow mural at Amma's crèche.

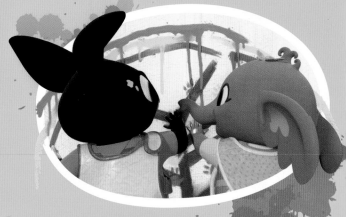

S is for Swing

Bing likes to play on the swing in the park. When Flop pushes Bing he can go really **high**. **Wheeeee!** It's lots of fun – but it's hard waiting for your turn!

T is for Talkie Taxi

Talkie Taxi is a **very noisy** taxi. Whenever you press her horn she talks! Bing and Sula like it **best** when they do the noises. Then Talkie Taxi can be an ambulance! **Neee-nawww, neee-nawww!**

Neee-nawww!

U is for Umbrella

When it **rains**, Bing and Flop have their own **special** umbrellas to stop them from getting **wet**. The rain **drip-drips** down the umbrellas, but Bing and Flop stay dry!

V is for Voo Voo

When Bing does a clumbo and **spills** Crispos on the floor it's time to get Voo Voo out. Voo Voo **cleans** up the mess in no time!

Voo voo!

W is for Wibbly-wobbling

The rope bridge in the park **wibbles** and **wobbles** when you walk across it. Pando thinks wibbly-wobbling is **lots** of fun!

X is for eXtra-crunchy carrots

Carrots are Bing's **favourite** food, and **extra-crunchy** carrots are the best. Bing gives Flop an extra-crunchy carrot to make him feel better when he's ill. Carrots make **everything** better!

Y is for Yellow wellies

Bing's yellow wellies are **perfect** for jumping in puddles. They keep his feet **warm** and **dry** while he plays outside. *Splish! Splash! Splosh!*

Z is for zzzzzz

ZZZZZ . . . it's Bing's bedtime. Flop has read him a story and now Bing is **tucked up** all cosy in bed with Hoppity Voosh. **Goodnight, Bing!**

My year with Bing

What a **busy year** it's been! Bing has...

Fed the ducks with Sula

Seen a digger with Pando

And grown **that much** taller!

This year, I have...

But his **favouritest thing** was putting on a show with all his friends!

But my favouritest favourite thing of all, was...

As well as...

What will you do next year, Bing Bunny?

Next year, Bing wants to...

Bake Ginger Bunnies

Without burning them!

Learn to hula-hoop like Coco!

And be a good friend

What do YOU want to do next year?

Next year, I want to ....

....

....

....

....

Bedtime Storymaker

Bing has had a **big** day, and it's nearly time for bed. But first, it's **storytime!** And you can help to tell this story! Look at the words and follow the story, and every time you see this ✱, **you** choose what happens next.

Got it?
Yup!

Once upon a time in ....

✱ a magical castle

✱ a giant skyscraper

✱ a little wooden house

✱ (where else can you think of?)

there lived a very busy nurse, who worked hard all day helping people.

One day, the nurse....

✱ saw something crash to the ground!

✱ saw something flash past the window...

✱ heard a quiet 'knock knock' at the door.

✱ (what else can you think of?)

The nurse went to take a look, and found a hoppy frog!

The frog said, "**Ribbit!** I'm not really a frog. I'm a superhero who flies all over the world helping people. But one day I flew too fast, and annoyed...

✱ a grumpy old witch

✱ a huge and hairy giant

✱ a scaly green dragon

✱ (what else can you think of – that's *really* scary?)

"...they got cross and turned me into a frog, but frogs can't fly like superheroes and I CRASHED out of the sky and hurt my leg!"

"Oh poor Froggy! I will help you," said the nurse. "First, let's put a plaster on your leg. There, that's better."

And then the nurse...

* sang a happy song (Which song was it? Can you sing it too?)

* gave the frog a big slippery hug! (Can you give your grown-up one too?)

* said 'FROGGY SOGGY SUPER DOO' three times (You try it!)

* (what else can you think of to make the frog feel better?)

And **puff!** the frog turned back into a superhero!

"Oh, thank you so much!" said the superhero. "Now I can go back to helping people."

"Hmmm..." said the nurse, "I help people too. Perhaps we could help people together?"

"That would be wonderful! Take my hand," said the superhero.

And together, the nurse and the superhero flew off to...

* a busy funfair

* a sunny beach

* the North Pole

* (where would you most like to fly to?)

...where they helped lots and lots of people!

The End

Goodnight, Flop!
Goodnight, Bing!